Networks

ALSO BY MARK DICKINSON

Tender Geometries

Mark Dickinson

Networks

Shearsman Books

First published in the United Kingdom in 2022 by
Shearsman Books
PO Box 4239
Swindon
SN3 9FN

Shearsman Books Ltd Registered Office
30–31 St. James Place, Mangotsfield, Bristol BS16 9JB
(this address not for correspondence)

www.shearsman.com

ISBN 978-1-84861-765-0

Acknowledgements
Some of these poems or versions of poems have appeared in
*Blackbox Manifold, Long Poem Magazine, Molly Bloom,
Tears in the Fence* and *Shearsman* magazine.

Contents

OUTLIERS

INELEGANT SPACE

SOUS-MASSA (LETTERS HOME)

Pattern Shock

Updraughts

(Fulmarus glacialis)

Love gapes—rubbed into emptiness, where the narrowing whiteness peels, rinsing the plexus at a verge of microns, reflecting so closely the pivoting feathers near the calm fidelity of touch. Seeing how the stiff wings share on horizon but steer the void. The tide cohabits with latent triesters; abbreviates in quiet. How land devoutly shelters through bare depressions the medicine of its distempers.

Red gape

(Cepphus grylle)

Tracing movements of water through the quiet rocky islands where indentations speak, as the wind strengthens and the water's presence regales the night. Even event switch prays uneven, where storm-splints-lullaby navigates the seep of the same shored orison.

Open country

(Circus cyaneus)

In a pre-thicket edged by selection we breathe the numbing distance of late autumn rain where the harrow fells seem to carry us down. Among the desperate acres the empty voyeur puffs at the wind, tempting enough to follow. "There's so much in the weather." Spectres rush like air, picking a pass through fields to field.

Holartic clade

(Corvus corax)

The Northern sky seems darker than usual, & the triumph of the darkness seems prehistoric with turbulent regressions. In the gloom of stress every instinct descends in to the Mitochondrial, & every word seems fitted like feathers around the throat. In a deep bowl made of twigs & sticks resting on a defenceless ruin, importance is represented by the *ultimate end*.

Between the Lores

'His eye is on the sparrow'
(Passer domesticus)

A small tree frequented with an additional i, where the caesura appears suspended between faith & thought. The circadian rhythm of activity is distributed among the worrying macerations of incarnated particles. Each sentience participates within a period entraining a sink. Once discovered, each sentence requires the addition of further thought. There is a cycle of light & dark & perhaps everything is threatened. The pine cone is a small endocrine among dynamic structures & not one of them is forgotten by God.

Wintering grounds

(Limosa lapponica)

Cast back to zones of benthic infauna, gathering heart & mouth
to the burrowing foot close to the anus in the grey-brown winter.
Settling is risk, where loop requires trading from the sori, which
liberates under a blue light, as the microscopic flocks the coast.

Loving

(Pagophila eburnea)

Leucistic remembrance declines with light toward the tender & frail, melting the familiar touch of a winter kindled in love. Seeing the sweetness of light & elegance issuing from a heart among declining ice where the sound of faults becomes over-sad, & may grow greater. Moss, lichens & seaweed, Love attending the errors; the strange melt sliding into the silent.

Radical desire

(Phalacrocorax aristotelis)

The advection of the infinite transports with bulk motion the object of the primitive enclosed within soft opacities clouding the cornea. Whether to negotiate the outward complexities or seek between the brilliance falling through the gentleness of a veil, even in outline the unthinkable forms in a space where the wind drops. In the realm of silence the symbol becomes impossible to speak. Perhaps in finitude of day's horizon, perspective recovers the infinite recurving from sheer perplexity.

Luminous darkness

(Vanellus vanellus)

The cloud conceals the incomprehensible behind the visible. Toward the invisible, approach speaks of a light trailing the broken. When history comes of age, universal truths anchor the extra-ordinary; hearing that the dark will speak of the light. Movement is [in] tension | where darkness, with intent, keeps them apart. In the darkness of night, feeling a presence, the crested plumes thread with equal care through coastal meadows.

At the state of the perfect

(Haematopus ostralegus)

How to approach the glorious or near the gentle situation, where embraces transform with great care, announcing low over the water, resisting threats or the violation of dignity.
How to read aloud or in circles held forwards & downwards. What is beautiful & various incline the gaze almost to torment. It is this night and purgation, thirst shouting to be heard. The pathless heights strange & remote settle like plovers.

Repugnant to accommodate

(Gallinago gallinago)

Imperfect affliction giving a note of violence flies away & finds no sweetness. On entering the narrow the inward darkness takes no pleasure from the trailing edge of snow. During the winter goodness works passively to go back home. Playful scars distort the wilderness. Divinity hides in the vegetation & is active at night. The crossing can be understood in many ways & also has a silent display. Whole events impact the field in a parody of likeness. Let it suffice to describe with imperfections.

Lens

(Columba livia)

Stretching foam to spin among the heavens where light's myth forms its stretches denting the eye along the ethics of matter back to a love of intricate echoes greying to quiet hills.

Track while scan

(Catharacta skua)

Slender wing distance to pattern shock of frigid 'Redstart' burning care, where mute experience neglects potassium in vagrant tenderness *brittle* to riot air.

As well as

(Corvus cornix)

Walks out of the still furze carrion stone its distant face couches
near the sea. To break apart nothing that you fail enchants me. In
flowers curled resistant brilliance. Falling apart I feel somehow.
Light in the afternoon mist, trying to be awkward, where the
difficult folds back its finishing touch, which notes of the hours,
the furthest proofs of prayer are nervous & unanswerable. Since
that time appal & smell the orchid, which is looking really nice.

Another story

(Pinguinus impennis)

There is another story straining behind a ghost. Yesterday it dragged across the grass a painful memory which dismantled the sun. In the dun light starry rhythms circumvent faithless arms. Everything here is happening quietly, & is mostly imperceptible. Parasitical dreams of no ending extract the loneliness from absent feathers. Gathering a sense of love from a hole of black earth is dark, dark, & everything is leaving.

Busking

(Cygnus olor)

A thoughtless act without comparison stills the wings tracing the bones edge to the bevelled indent of love. Where a small return meaning death ships the stern sea whets & a tooth edged clot tills the voice, dressing the mouth with empty apologies which answer the terror shaking the inside out. Crying quietly behind the broken current, under the rose of other symbols, knotted in the light of beaten skin, the boredom of detonations deface the broken lines which stammer to p r o n o u n c e dam age s tumbling t h rough m o u t h f u l s of h u r t.

Cytochrome

(Falco tinnunculus)

For Jamie Lawrence

You swallowed enough to keep from meaning beauty; believing in the emptiness of meat, showing itself in a monoxide of griefs that your spirit inhabits in the arctic black. The day is conflicting. A melody that tastes of summer watches you like the efforts of rain. When the image becomes too much, turn away. My veil became clear in thoughtless transparencies with indiscriminate mouse dust.

Strains

(Anthus pratensis)

~~Every 3 metres | a post | three strained wires | contemplate straining~~
~~where eyes | walk | mixing with the grasses | in a field at nightfall~~
~~grasses almost invisible | land | Sea close enough to touch |~~

With interest

(Larus marinus)

"You helped with nothing & are *selfish*!"; the tomatoes have *Phytophthora*, meaning *ruin*. The summer became a spring & spring was winter. The price of kerosene is 62.4p a litre (happiness and heating are like synonyms). The price of kerosene was 51.3p a litre. If you don't pay the balance in full, we'll allocate the balance to the highest interest. Tomorrow will not. Please see the default section. After tomorrow I hope to be a *shellfish* harvester. I wrote these lines around percentages so you don't need to pay much interest.

Change mitigation

(Calidris maritima)

The use of networks to encourage collective behaviour can be playfully dramatic, or softly so. We assign decisions to different mental accounts, 'priming' 'nudges' even in sleep. Darker than Dunlin the cupped pools tremble with glittering. This is light of the mind. The tree engages within the MINDSPACE model. Learned regarding is adapted to next time & the design of information & form remains awkward. The grey-coloured waterside lips the beautiful, engraving the terrible with vanishing attributes. Tomorrow the sky lowers, concealing the interventions suggested here, where the sea breathes a warming homicide.

Escape response

(Aurelia aurita)

I am exhausted. Sequential hermaphrodites hang like dew free from the sensation of weight, & feel themselves among currents of misuse. Empty links of space gifted to notes of glitter sparkle the nerve-net, as gentle endeavours swim.

Reduction from the primitive

(Semibalanus balanoides)

Modifications surround a series of overlapping wonders that close when threatened. In the ocean a distant stretches across a breathing movement responsive to a broad unknown, while quietly the drifting instars moult toward complexity. There is only a trace of primordial valves on the umbones of whiteness peopled in stars. On each side of the galactic tide invisible reflections drag across my body, making two little folds of skin that burn like a comet.

Remnant wild

(Salmo salar)

A falling river. spreads desire. moults. small ships in the night.
MEAT. bringing hymns. from egg to market. through developing.
Eye. mesh. alloy of netting. lash. because the maximum sustainable
yield competes with Canthaxanthin. & the colour of the wild.
potent. lipid. scavenging synthesis. to ease-less similes. of lab-scale.
protein. whispering. post-hatch. life. drawn to unrelated questions
of crystal disposition on the retina. cosmetic. transgenic marine.
laid her exposure. to draw-back critically. *'bone to the sea'* –

A word of Love

(Alauda arvensis)

The hills are not irritable as crumbling promises starve among a famine of kisses, where a secrets love travels upon an old wound & beats down animal with coins, becoming the skull of failing in a forest of pieces, as every tremble spitting among the shrubs tugs and tears like a violent insult outlined by a comforting sorrow. Between gorse & the lark begging in the desert, come drink the rap of analysis in the dark mind, & hunt down a purpose because of death.

"Sometimes we screw things up for the better."

(Salix hookeriana)

Pissing against the wind at night without sleep burning the mouth in the garden settled for a perch. Unexpected combinations of love formless & empty batter the sky. Attachable fill hooked to a crackle switches the ecstasy to a chosen exterior breaking across the willows.

Death of a Naturalist

(Tipula paludosa)

Haphazard & peculiar, hung on the patterned ceiling like a giant mosquito. Your slender form trapezes on deciduous legs, harnessed to glass \/ wings that precariously hover; your strange eyes suggesting the supernatural, peer through stages of putrefaction in search of your opposite. I watch you, late in darkness, tracing the ethics of a lifetime through abdominal segments, into those dark squadrons of headless tubes, slicing neatly, through the roots.

Micro patches

(Sagina subulata)

Unity endures its patch of habitation primed to adaptive rapidity trapped along a path, trembles through nodes of darkness, conveying sorrow toiling through love. Infinite persistence, along a graph of finite resistance – groans the thresholds network, departs to micro-patches thinning to a graft of solitude.

This with a fly in my mouth

(Drosophila melanogaster)

I'm not particularly interested in sickness or your fondness for burning animals. I do not wish to hurt you, or fill the throat with panic. Every night spaces close, cough into the edgeless pale envelopes beautifully broken against love. Utter loneliness between me and the promise of happiness. Stillness changes the light with new forms of violence edging your mouth. I reach for another image strained through the knot-holes of the heart polished abnormally, & watch the trembling shapes the wind informs. Seated between apologies on the edge of coping, interspecific confusion moves through the grass.

Sketches of loss

(Crex crex)

Contortions of audio decentralise a careful malignant whorl at a thrust of love upsizing the slight dissatisfaction. Entrapment particulates a vein of resignation grafted to paralysis. Whole wakes of convalescence dream a century prostrate across self interest. Sketches of loss pretty with limitation mark eaves of night terraced with bias. Immunity of delectation summons the crash of tree. In singing waters a shade of fluttering is best historical; even so, I think I am startled by the relevance.

Baits of happiness

(Picea sitchensis)

Patterns sometimes seem a view of neat illuminations brittle with warming influence. I wonder after a thousand oppositions of wakeful spite, if to know the impressions of intimacy through the interest of tensions is integral to the inter-connected systems of feeling. The copper light at work in the dun particles has charged the threnody of driftwood through its journey from tree. Defacing the fostering beams, I blunt the mouth with a packet of distraction. You look at me, scattering this course filthy with eternity.

Decapitated theology

(Crataegus monogyna)

Broken land half-frozen with permeance wet with work among Alder, the long think tuning the earth before time meant industry. Critical Birch gnawed like the zeal of puzzles flashing the mind with reasons I can't stop to analyse. Community of minor things, the native horizon hung in the ordinary, fall-filled with the energy of an acre. Beginning the mountain plants a spire of ponder to things, the greater need of exposures. Turn behind wisdom the burden of snow. I know that I am laid in grass watching a lesson in leaderless frustration. Circumstance that only pines, looks toward the sky & finds it good.

Free

(Betula pubescens)

Regrettable, dazzlement, compassion compressing submerged spaces of supremacy. Confusing fragrance with whiteness, the ill-lit mystery cramped into the slighter shade. The original pair planting itself like logic, trailing to sing the difference; labouring against them. I am amazed, periodically, to see the character burr its surge; the driftwood logs. He became a giver, his share of September sun. I know & feel the contradiction among the debris of trees.

OUTLIERS

Soiled

i

Bee spattered rundown
fading hover pit
lovingly drenched in shit

Backlit scene stripper
of sullied ruin
in morning gladness

Flood mingled heroes of
timothy dripping tattered
threadbare she-

aves the honest squalor
promised to a spirit stained
with harm

spit whispered to addled
throes punky with capital
the sodden grime

whose myths record what I
have done   tied up in trust

these opaque throats of gods
align dis-
tasteful sacrifice.

*

Balls deep screaming
your unwanted
speculum

insert flood mingled diatribe
swallowing the ashes where I
believe in

violating rights/ stretching
down fist clamour/ streaming
love

in our rugged cell ass-
ault in the grey grass
rimming the crust of

banality

*

Experience the front bursting
into tears at the dreary inter
course

of human darkness
degrading the joy
of deep forms

sweating the golden stream
after the mind is blown
crossing the ditch

our

ass

ets hitched upon the moon
and turn again to itch our
deep ecology.

ii

Deep soiling eclogues
franchise of capital
snorting prismatic residue
soiling the dark past-
oral its sweet grime up-
skirts on stony paths
refreshing its lustre in the wet.

iii.

hear me out, trying to be kind with
words, but the rains tormentil. No
work these days, strange and suffering
fall on me, then in the eye, where living
growth pursues its end sent down with
my file.

Micro-Tree

Our analysis provides both examples of 'socialist' and 'capitalist' tendencies of mycorrhizal networks. In several cases small seedlings obtained more benefit (in terms of biomass gain) compared with the larger plants that established the mycorrhizal networks, pointing to socialist tendencies [...] However, there are also several examples which show that small seedlings receive proportionally the same or even less benefit from networks as larger plants. In terms of total biomass gains then, the larger plants thus benefit more from mycorrhizal networks, pointing to capitalist tendencies.
—Marcel G. A. Van Der Heijden and Thomas R. Horton

In protein channels the carriage of spontaneity alights on opportunity, outsourcing a resource through passive cotransport. This cooperative dynamic labours beyond the threshold of the singular, dispersing in its stead, intelligent codependents, as a strategy of nurture within array.

If hope mutates along transformative corridors, what conveys of its presence may invoke the terms of its intimacy. Parasitism may be a nub of the complex, and spoke around the hub of its catchment, as strained horizons migrate between genomes of similarity and difference, sharing a glyph dependence, which could state along its remit a counter, granulating the instance of its straining.

As a driver for coexistence, dynamic strategies trade across terms of difference, facilitating positive interactions among reciprocal exchange. Irrespective of status, roots of difference advance molecular dialogue through community dynamics, threading networks of new meaning. One of the many keys to facilitation, relates to co-occurring nurture, recycling spatial culture, for the benefit of the social networks at play within divergent roots.

Low (leaves) Moment

i

I do not fully understand
these leaves and their low moment of inertia
or the pattern of veins and the tiny bones
fitted with the impulse to travel;
there simply isn't enough
sunshine, (gas exchange or light capture)
entering through the open stomata,
knowing the warning signs
but editing the pain.

I've become accepting of inhumanity
schooled by the market
through the nerves that travel the brain.
The surface morphology mostly quiet
and the mechanical motion which, could be useful
to the superhydrophobic structure
concerned with the properties of men,
quickly grows in an uncertain   ratio
attempting to think the essence of god.

ii

In the winter when the tree was tree-less
I remembered the aggregates and the photogenic quality of the larynx
and in grouping the object similarities of our orifices
I noted, the pitted lenticels
while failing to note the age of each clone.
Perhaps in the new light of tomorrow
my thoughts won't echo
and the world and its layers
will no longer be recognisable.

Today, I dug in the rain again and watched the deductive system
          with impotence
neither bothered about the caustic nature of lime
or the continuity of each individual mix.
I changed my mind, but couldn't change my circumstance.
This demonstration of the gap between,
which happened when the ear was windowless,
I read as a combination of micro and nano structures,
established in the early developmental stages
that remained specifically dependent on the reader's own position.

iii

There are many ghosts
and many recognitions,
in the valley crossing itself, I wait alone
among the litter, another
northern sound on the edge
of the moor; dwelling in humiliations
aimed at my weakness, which represent
the trade of Freud and the degrees
of separation in the historical hour of this personal damp.

Where I have leaves, white into the dark
goes echoing some familiars, fluttering like
the twinkling flat of an angle, which almost
to silence—backs to its origin
stemmed from a quaking whisper
in the vertical cells; I to its slights of separation
into chambers between, where we feel the days
and the venation in parallels leaves
into the open space to pore the light.

iv

Softly now, without disinterest avowing the refuge of
stone, but cautious of the limit crossing between
decisions, liberating the gift from beneath the wavy divide
among the saproxylic insects, guided through
the negative shadow to the outer side of being,
which we admit to absolutely, or, not at all. Out
in the garden, the dioecious sphere corrected
by neutrality—such remains the question
bordered by the thinnest of moss which edges this deep.

I to its wish, stays sudden, strays tranquil,
weeping aspen to a lichen of cover.
Patterned by thoughts made angular,
among pieces of starlit catkins, with tiny
seeds floating down from a crown,
to a question which is not self-
evident, walking controversially in
salted turbulence, scorched at the edge of
being and pierced by estrangement.

Olav's Wood

We sought love among those narrow trails,
the lived light curving between the glittering
wood moss, and the wind burnt wynds where patience
grew selective through a force that gathered
to a common feather, touching the lifting
feature of how we came to the touch
of a frizzled pincushion. Becoming a gift
where we would dwell, knowing the Holarctic
elegance colonising the duration
of what we felt, and sought at the threshold
slant to the water. Estranging bitter
interruptions lifted from the dazzling
frown, notched to a distant twist of cruelty
that violence heats. At the side, we stopped:

before a silken retreat, where the water
of the burn/ split/ into the silver
carpet of a woven orb/ a rhizoid
drawn to its shade, among tea-
pots nesting—sung to the heart, where the fragile
laughter's treading the love to the audible
Crake, blessed in the slant/ light that implicates
faith, and greets us, inclining the elegant
bristle among the spring that counts the syl-
lables of discovery. Feeling the earth
in the glittering, which fade down in-
to the comforting hint of a beauteous
narrow, whose star water carries the softest
notes of happiness, to harmonise the tree
side of this temple, where the world grows
better than
before.

Upturned Sun

A low forest, no more than 20 centimetres high, located on the miniature banks of a burn. Petalled, on hairless stems—cordate leaves, dark green; the single flowers signal a grounded sun. Between falling stones, habitats form, dismissing neglect. Among small stands of whorls, linear branches spread toward cleavers, their hooked hairs clambering beneath the knotted twist of Fuchsia, in its roofless byre, spreading into stands of stems with stinging juice.

There is a generative span of music opening to the quiet of the sea. Connecting unspoken distance, administering the momentary hint of freedom, which finds its own moment, in a whisper of possibility.

Quiet tolerance presents beneath the wide blunt leaves, slows motion, unpurling the caustic diadem in the shade. There is a hurtful uncertainty among a necessary quiet, altogether essential; being careful not to overemphasise the spoil, or overstate the taxing questions, which exhort a necessary plea for the fraying remains.

Angelic (kneads) Umbellifer

'A good many south country plants find their way to Orkney amongst agricultural seeds, but very few survive beyond a season, and probably not more than one or two have been acclimatised. On the other hand there is a marked difference when seeds are brought from the north. On the banks near the village of Pierowall, Westray, and on the roadside, there is a plant, Archangelica officinalis, which leas no doubt been brought with fishing, smacks from the Faroe Isles, where it is abundant. It is thriving splendidly, and producing strong healthy seed. It is not native in Britain.'

Shrunk to its need, the hybridity of wild encasing through gift those specular intervals of nodal foreshortening to the secular kneads of ground; low distancing, between leaf nodes and the dense splay of the crown. Where the leafy chlorophyll crouched to resistance, diverts to a thickness of grace. Couched along latitudes, each cell of nurture stems the over-reach to a thicknesses apex. Restraining the upright through a cleft of occupancy, where risks of height sway before prostrate increments of impotence. Such potent respite before a paradigm will opportune in the store of density, recoverable in this open extremity. Aligned to succession compressed to a hollow, where depth retains an hereditary posture within a reach specific to its niche. Hunkering fit withstanding the jettisoned, from opened drops of ocean-sharp, bitten-at-sore. Graft to its draft, each leafy dimension marks visible the open constraint: imparts within a bounded condition the measure of restraint. Any faint stands will be at loss, as any over-height of obduracy marks frail upon florescence. Such stranding makes in its specular increments the standing of offer, lessening by trials beside a trail on this coastal path. Salt dash galling, which moderates the song of its outburst, raising the annuity, razing the quiet solemnity; kneading the future, given to porrection, to see what gives. Fleshing site-base with a slope-flush of promise; shifting the climax with pronounced fluctuations in its northern range. Wind-belt to over-arching— supine: therophyte generating radical inheritance, whose continuity is the measure of concentrated patience, which marks between the morphological strands, the terms of its angelic stands.

Stone Pine Meditation

'That we love as best we can' —Charles Causley

One

In a mornings ripple the momentum of stone, its breath of veins
flexing a space between a moment of slow reparations. After that
shore of difference, sleek cells slope along a needle's propensity,
like marginal wakes cast doubtful; each tone-care of evening
awakens to thoughtful trimmings of time.

Two

A needle dropped through abstracts of silence, becomes hard,
like intractable sorrow, as stone sets canopy & shape sets evening,
reaching to detail & wonder. This love-cast needle sways into
bracts of parasol, with strain & patience & patterns of vertical
textures stretched between rain & reverence.

Three

Hard ache, ligatures the pattern of age, inscribed with 'essence',
nearness with care softly grounding the distance. No small
wonder in pairings of delicate stiffness, the openness between
the soft liturgy of pine. We stand in the fill of directions & open
in pleats the depth of "happy", its remarkable spoke—in-breathe
the token lent.

Four

Heart strain permeates division en-route to careful leaning, cones its likeness piercing of learning "stone". Happy in a notch of shore, softly sharing a forage of beams, where sound to pin-wing-silence goes to a pine-song-graft to its pairing; all sorrow to its hitch, now that the gradient of ground counters the lean with its camber.

Five

From a light of colour close to night, small hands inquire of form the prospect of tomorrow. The coned homing of habitation rests naturally in palms. Amazement reveals the conical, embrace unfurling its spiral between fingers & "nut?". How eyes deliver this simple perplexity, as resinous acts clinging to a taste of memory, emerges without irony, as sprouts of playful origins forge into gifts of kind.

Six

Night-maker star-slung between different darks, turn time with the inert breath stretched between the vaulting shadows. Sweet carapace! – The lone clasp of stone flutters its stay where the firm ridge of pine angles untidily between the veil.

Inelegant Space

Personalised to Mean Nothing

We were happy and careless or just careless? I'm tired of splitting hairs & I'm always reminded of dark polythene. There is no good way to say this, but the sorrow you spoke of made me laugh, and at this point, it really was good to say goodbye. It's nice out, but cold, or not nice, if you don't like cold, but still nice. A small wreck of emotion transforms to disappoint. Small particles lodged between teeth. The beauty of love is, it can be personalised to mean nothing of Love. Forks in the road are not as problematic as knives. Sometimes when I dream I watch an old man stoop and pick a golden leaf out of a rusty old bucket. Just for the record my eyes really bring out the sky. Those small clouds which aren't for everyone have beautiful curves. Though I prefer a wisp or a furred thread, but if this view comes up for sale, I'll open it up to fluffs & ribbons. Ribbons & fluffs. In certain settings anyone on the gender spectrum can be in the minority. She held my hand, gave me some pills and told me to look at her secrets. In another room he did the same. The smell was confusing. If he focused on more delicate themes there would be more profundity in his use of colour. She has a masculine quality. I am certainly open to your suggestive manipulation which I think is remarkably natural.

Open to Awkward

Given the current climate and economic uncertainty I am open to passive suggestions. If I'm honest about the things I think about, you'll probably leave. Poetry is a flash of Lapwings. I like dragging you by the hair, it makes me feel better. When I'm alone I think about pink glitter and Vaseline, when I'm with somebody I think I'm better off alone. Nature poetry is a fetish of voyeuristic abuse. I want to own a hawk and condition it. In the rain I will insert the word *'Respect'* because it is necessary. When I was younger I watched a man punch a rabbit so many times its eyes became dislodged from the sockets. How it lived through this experience I'm not sure. Once desensitised you can get so many pleasures from so many things; you can even get paid for them. In this factory you can abuse pigs. In this house you abused me. Forestry soils are complex and climax vegetation is possibly rarer than diamonds on the foreskin of the master. Some poets are childhood fiddlers. I am skirting the edges and my wrist is limp, but have a good gag threshold which means I'm open to awkward objects. At the dentist some people have a hyperactive reflex where anxiety and fear can flow down the throat. I used to believe in something. I've extracted a perch of wires and evicted the birds. This brought me to Facebook, and the hottest full-length images of jockeys with fibreglass criss-cross shafts, gold ferrules and caps. I googled human bridle and was reduced to the *status of animal* and taken *to the town*. To enforce silence I adjusted the iron bar in the hollow tree. Its song is slightly melancholy but pleasing. Retreating into a machine gun salvo the voice has become rough and hoarse. Tomorrow will be succeeded by clusters of small red berries.

Friend Request

A bald man dreams of hair and wakes up disappointed, clouds are no substitute and the wilderness, if it can be called that, is problematic. When I dress like a thrush I constantly quiver. With each new corruption the monotony of self pervades the snowcapped blossom. The words, "I love you" are vivid in autumn, but I'm not prepared to have a discussion on the subject at this time. I opened the curtains so the sun could shine on the righteous. In my garden (note the possessive) I saw a blackcap. Snow buntings gather in the field and I intrude on their moment, they take flight, settle and watch me from a safer distance. Vegans should pay attention to sources of organic phosphorus; origins can be problematic. Corrosive Economics are pervading the tundra in search of delirium. As a child I was beaten so badly my skin turned red, blue, black, green, yellow. In the present the trauma of force seeps into microscopic rainbows which become vivid and deep in winter. Behind the force of a coal shovel lay intent. Happiness is complicated and requires a sheltered spot with protection against hard borders. Everything seems perpetually messy. But the plough has shaped the soil so the structure is new. If you tilt your head ever so slightly to the left, you'll see complexity through simplicity. I am over whelmed by facts and figures but underwhelmed when trying to participate. Only scripted narratives make sense. I hover over the water in a pattern of light & dark. Show me your cliches and I'll buy you a drink [slow breathing, muffled sounds – yet audible]. The path is overgrown with mixed forage grasses and Wordsworth's *mutable finitude*, it leads to a theory of abandonment, which is incomplete, leaning toward a resolution of entanglement, stretched from the Holocene into this relational depth. As light rips gently into the future it does so with impressive fluidity. Small stones dark with rain. I trespass at your window & reimagine your past, my intrusion becomes a fantasy of apparitions drowning in a water feature. Nothing makes me happy but, "I love you".

Unsubscribe

Tears ambush the central reservation and I'm not sure what to do about it. Living ethically is proving to be expensive, but with enough money 'self-sufficiency' becomes an option. Subscribing to the law of attraction I focused on a wind turbine and the universe brought me a large colourful holographic windmill to stick in the sand. I don't like cutting myself, but occasionally I will punch myself repeatedly in the face. Honesty is the best policy, unless it's the worst. Now I have your attention I want to mention urban acidification and tree adaptability. I am dreaming of a scrub savannah at the tree-limit, where islands of crooked wood stretch the horizontal through apical termination, as resource gains exceed the losses by the thinnest of margins. There are many lessons to surviving at the extremes of tolerance. Thin calls with a touch of orange flutter momentarily. I have thoughts on violence as the intellectualised or creative use of excess. I grow many types of flower but primrose (vulgaris) is native, yet should not be considered an indicator of ancient woodland. I find the appearance of dwarf willow in the verges curious. I'm inclined to snatch small animals from the surface of water, but focus instead on the sunshine yellow of the daffodil and the cold north wind that desiccates. When I was little he hit you, I blamed myself but the lupins which aren't native bring fresh optimism to the colour blue. Lupins in Iceland are becoming invasive, but today I want to focus on a positive and the efficiency of interaction between different nodule bacteria in relation to the variability of nitrogen fixation. But realistically I'm more likely to follow an alarm call against humans that's a dry rasping scream among intermittent hints of blue & yellow.

Rioting in Comfort

I dressed in a party frock rioting through the small affections of conformity with melancholic pre-assembled speech bubbles that made me feel awkward. In the living room a new theatre of wilderness paraded its evergreens through pre-existing harmonies of colour. At the limit of love trailing through binary stars I brushed against anthers strained by distance like a falsetto bark.

Legacy

A legacy of national obsession contributes to a future impossible to recognise. Small distressing signals wrapped in coins splinter across the quirks of desirability, & a green-screen seminar on liquid JOI gathers the rebate from our collective intimacy. At dusk fearless cries script the mournful almost in flight. Lost among these white flowers, indents of carbon integrate a risk of maintenance, with the precision of anthropological uncertainty.

Exposed to a World of New

In a field of grass types, a whole bird with a twisted wing, lays perfectly still. The heavy build unmistakably pied, stiffens. The white bar across the throat, diminishes to an accepted fact, flattening into a small clump of patience, which becomes an emblem of resignation. If perfection has stillness, the climax of its display is local, and resembles the empty vacancy of a throat feeding on the incisions of the irreversible. In clotted voice, the shape of abrasion, transitions the deadlock, and the cost of movement through the pantheon of macro-economics is accounted. In the distance, the quite noise of the remarkable, gently announces itself over time. In the fields library, the pattern of travellers becomes a record, a fungal drape of populations across a range of industries, fraught with control. If there were pretty flowers and not much grass, perhaps the register of meaning would be different.

Delete-Delete

Now that the music's on standby and nobodies home I want to rub myself in a new kind of sadness. Where anxiety accompanies the fresh bright empty through paradisiacal incompleteness to a place that's simply not robust enough to pirouette through the crisis, or shimmy through its glittering deletions. At each emptying injunctive, the sweet vowel meadows and consonants of wilderness spread to inelegant blank space. Where the surface of eyes mirror scraps of yesterday, painting the coastal frescoes with denatured love and little fears that stalk the landscapes monotonous tracts, stain the harmonies with glimmering distress and consume to a fraction.

Out of tune

Leaning against a tiny discreet petal, our window on the obvious sounds like a mistimed overture accompanied by the prising of metal. In ministered convulsions modified in revelations of mist gathered on the summit of climate, we drift through portals of glitter into gutters of transport discharged to disappointment. Our Inserts of fetish found then lost, link back to a status which continued to reinvent itself post-death. How in this sphere of porous calamities, did graceful inserts subject to submissive tropes, become gilt fondled hems denatured & forever reinvented? Nothing of this music screens behind the glass of unwelcome, now that the sill of margins is selective mute and the cost of belonging, embossed in digits, balances the snow white purity on the unseasonal sheet.

Sous-Massa

(Letters Home)

Argan tree

My friend, we are in a landscape of ocean & semi-desert. In the afternoon dust blows across space & bald Ibis stroll along the edge of things. The river is dry & filled with unwanted transparencies. The sun will not rise, so we must learn to swim in the dark.

A friend has sold my copy of *Les Fleurs du Mal* & during Ramadan takes cocaine. He tells me that the woman in the other room will tend to the Parisians need, caressing his nerves. I leave in a blue taxi & a seated man places the point of a small blade gently at my sternum; we must carefully tread our difference.

I have a copy of Duncan Wu's *Romanticism*, I sit on a stone facing the western ocean & feel the breath of the desert wind. I am introduced to an English man from the Arif mountains who likes young boys. In the evening I watch the scorpions, climb freely on boulders, hang precariously, or scramble the Atlas watching the sun.

There is a Man in the village who calls me "Fish & Chips", we do 'business' in a windowless room, where a picture hangs, framed by candles, he says, "I do not like, your kind". In another part of the village an old man behind glazed windowless eyes begs for cigarettes. He is vague & clings uncertainly to the present.

A friend from Brittany is suffering from psychosis, he will not eat, but we drink together. It is light, the water cool & we float, waiting for displacement, drifting through halos & twinkles of uncertainty. The movement is, magical, each chambering envelope astonishing; the fine detail of air, the intimate compression. We are watching & discovering, recovering—the soluble instance of compassionately dissipating beauty.

The truth is, I'm pleased that I have little but happiness to give. A tortoise in the wild, deception & sleep. Tomorrow I will take the bus to the place where children draw small fingers across small throats. Make transactions. Sometimes I feel welcome in the spiny protective shelter of *Argania spinosa* rooted in calcareous permanence, which seems, hardly true.

I have found a question forming modernity in the *Quran*. The mountain & the profit reaching for the tangible. In Tangier the fine tuned placement of a broken splinter in the heart. In lee of the Cape, Europe quieter, distant.

Ground Squirrel

Hello my friend, I am in the presence of a Barbary ground squirrel, it is wild & a 'delicacy', a consternation of sand & bark. I must take the time to notice the wild & hasten my pace to capture a glimpse of the Barbary partridge. I notice a bald ibis delicately close to absence. In Jordan, they fight over water. In Marrakesh, the foreign hunter has shot too many Turtledoves. My throat is dry & I am thankful for the currency of plastic. I need to hide in the foothills of mountains & learn the politics of water.

During the day I watch smoke from burning plastic rise out of the semi-wetland of the yoga camp, where they are reconnecting & seek the fragrance of balance. I take a walk through blind paths of beautiful glass, & pretty melted blocks of colour, to see the thick backed mullet sifting beyond. Everything is conserving the limitless loss in the sun's commodity. Alone, & close to the edge, things seem desperately real.

Scorpion

I should write something, perhaps about a DIY landscape made from a piece of fabric draped over a bulb smouldering with darkness.

I will write about Scorpions: *Androctonus mauritanicus, Buthus elmoutaouakili, Hottentota gentili.* I spend hours scrambling among stone in undisciplined disturbance, seeking defiant myths with the plate dark armour of economy.

I am in love with dreams, the small bend in the empty river playful with fear. At night, between narrow passageways, distant registers of delicate entropy pass among exotic desires in tones of prophets, where we dream a god of water & think back to the turning of stones

> & the spines on the branches
> & the almost crimson
> succulent green
> masters' of scarcity
>
> & the maritime succulence
> & the black wheatear
> with the spiny desert
> darkling beetle

sliding beyond the nights'—cold, dry, aggregate of extremes; the dust bowl steppes, grazing the sparseness & in revision, the writing of something—detuned.

Oil Beetle

What is it this dry lyric?
an old benevolent coda

comfort as opiate,
the dark water's
numb taxonomies of loss

the red-striped oil beetle
morphed into sun,
the mottle of personae

rich in aposematic
declarations of toxic
behaviour

calm flotilla of quiet
hid in suffocation
help to prise

me / apart
(cocaine shadow/
dark fire)

the cost of each
stunning loss
a cool mimicry

Chameleon

There will be no peace while the motives are base. The labyrinthine fortress of walls, hides me from my motive, a fifth limb in a coiled spiral, the sun in muted tones.

According to circumstance the blue hours deepen the cells in the skin to the presence of ambush, slow & rhythmic, sparse in foliage.

Happiness is sedentary, or contorted extreme; the gait over ground, the bush concealed, the sound at night, they shape the limbs, or spend the night completed.

I spend the evening in happy deconstruction in a ground cavity; the permanence incomplete. Vulnerable & threatening, like a different place, my mouth projected to the mood of colours, teases apparitions into catatonic infancy from what is not.

Anime Field

High Strangeness

Unblock origin (all by itself) in gravity
or radioactive bizarre, released into a
state of enemies. I do not mean, I
think, in terms of high-

strangeness, the last lament for a last
snowball, colonised by something
redeeming from the past. If you are into
lab-testing, dark westerns or the life of

cannibals, yet totally bored, just say something
"weird" and point at the stars. I am staking
out the beach for insight to the perfect and logical
solution to love, twisting the pacts of occasional

demons, as a victim falling asleep because
life is a business. I'm not synchronised, just
sick and sad, bitchin' my way out of the net
more boring than Thor. Don't worry! I am

a purist, encoded with variable bit
rates and out of sync with the chemistry of
stuff. After this generation is gone, I want to
masturbate with love, watching a future in mono-

chrome, speaking at empty universities and having
a great experience. I will still update my personal
but may become a dolphin, it's hard to say
"really" but *I do want to* "imprint" mayhem

in my public chat, and enjoy the Stonehenge Apocalypse.

Live Stream

Command me or message me knock
me for a limited time to bring back
happiness, confusing inaction
grazing the past.

Like damage to stay at speed, &
love, to alter, the fantasies projecting
appearance to die & find unable
the present misleading way.

Hentai vs. Farmcore

1

A picture of loose dreams yearns without disorder
its hybrid wording not consenting to distress.

Consider the environment, a shaft of enlarged light
streaming organically through sunny fields of abnormal harmonies,
engorged in the ruffles of pleasing stalks, by loving hands caressed.

2
Trembles of imperfection,
mouth incomprehensibly

thoughts of a dangerous mind, resolved
to force. The beautiful is terribly faint, the sacred

pleasures of a toy, at the centre
of broken peace, heavy with power.
You own the quiet of the world

The beautiful gust swelling with force,
the trouble of a fly,

precious bones out of the sea
dimensions which enter me.

Expression of fandom

Excellent!—but the work is 'garbage'
& you almost made me
depressed. I've been waiting a long time
for brilliance, for anything

deemed okay, but the sentence is
negligent & if you value the craft
take care of the biome
but don't use the words

you could have *been*,
growing
in logic
eating sweat
in a corner of

heartbreak
cramped,
as a man
banking
regret,

every night
your animate
disappointment

diving into perishables
and tossed in the *quick*

nut of pain
between the *real* talk
and the *truth*
tucked into the
laundry

of the mediocre
adoring the sweet
suck of 'no
matter'

watching the stock
pile of forgotten minutes
and smelling the stupid
sauce

of button lint
its yellow lick
dumb-
struck with unintentional ass.

(peace & solitude)

We are still here in the quiet city
still around the last bits of unanswered prayers,
inside the vacant horror, *like a mad germ*
staring into a paperback fiction too far gone.

Our hurt—breathing & breaking
into enclosures of mind
vesting the 'ugly'
in cycles of grieving

where we are numb to the cells of kind
and twisted apart by an unkind
thirst. Our fever burns, afraid
of the deep; a pelvic bomb, out of

the details. Silence blooms
on the gospel of eardrums.
We hurt like that, a rift of consequence,
freed for a moment by a drift of flowers.

bondage & profit

It is nonconsensual the fields perimeter
& subject to a force of influence
piercing & gripping tautness
in a sequence, stretching entitlements
stapled to resistance; chaste in tension,
the surreal bovine, bracing
an eyelet to an icon's submission.

Imagine power spaced between
numerous bindings, fixed
with variation & permanently wired
to proteins of dominance,
galvanised by a feeling
of control, with differing
motivations bound to metal.

Subsidised without
concern, incubating
long fiscal chains,
in details of tenure, fantasy
fielding each economic block
of green desert, its weight
of green yield links petty

tokens of inconsequential
wool, to the dark sided mill.
Fences of inappropriate
desire compassionate still
at a rate, of not quite
understanding
the obvious. The old
standardised story about
the franchise of tradition, a cornerstone
of life, thriving the multi-year

but gripped in bonds of hatred,
a split injection of scale, re-wilding
its own fantasy, a pastoral joke
ejaculates on the udder side of

allocations, bound to its yoke
freely rebuilding the fortunate
from the mood of opinions,
not well executed. I love this need
to die, stripping the idol
broke on the karaoke of future
and skinned for the interest,

enhancing, but not convincing
enough to save the predictable
pleasure of glorious disappointment,
that depicts the unlikable benefits.
It is funny how the matching allocation
continues to frame the prominent
in calcified comfort.

block chain exit

Cut block on exit, time edges to black folds of cloud-rain intending my love. Could it be like our dream vagueness soldered to the shadow of a forest, subtracting green urges with unsparing past?

Tracing impossible night, slender devotion enfolding my love block, kissing thread breath to ear-charm. Love's pictured petal prickles the detail, stands prompted, doubts, cannot only, breath, since I for constellation exit the mind.

Songs in the aftermath fall apart and the resident implants longing. This is where, this enjoyed, that would alarm, exit in chain.

()

I discovered the exit, allowing for contact, sourced from imperfections. The predator in a quest for nitrogen digresses its relevance, walking with open orifice through other scenic paths.

Strain in-forms, forming mislabels, where the sunlight picks through the dust and the ghost of the present, unique in separation, clouds this mornings wire of sunlight. Stripped from the natural as it all recedes.

The waters' expand, and I tend to the stories anthropocentrically, a timestamp on the illegible. Blocks are chained together and the periphery species exit the block.

()

You scent the pathetic involute, the sound soft in leaf hush, the dark lick hunting a petal. Strange music, marginal music, word life or magic splint its pillow cleft in block, they keep only the proof-of-worth infused in dusting leaf.

North Sea

I am constantly reminded of the sedimentary
layers of the past, the politics of national
obsession and consumables, as pretty flotillas collected
to decorate fragile sand castles of the mind.

We are stood in the sea debating
the rise of climate anxiety and eating
the battered fish from an unknown source
which drowned in efficiency.

You collect the litter of the complacent
and cloud the emptiness with enchantment,
you are dosed with a pharmacopoeia of wonder
and pick among the sea worn plastic

'indicators', a sign, sea rise, discarded sand
castles and the dead. There is wonder
in the enchantment of litter, the refuse
of facts which decorate the castles of mind.

www.ingramcontent.com/pod-product-compliance
Lightning Source LLC
Chambersburg PA
CBHW020213090426
42734CB00008B/1055